DANCE
LIKE A
FLAMINGO

Moira Butterfield

Illustrated by Claudia Boldt

EDITIONS

Published in 2020 by Welbeck Editions

An imprint of Welbeck Children's Limited, part of Welbeck Publishing Group.

20 Mortimer Street, London, W1T 3JW

Text © Moira Butterfield 2020
Illustrations © Claudia Boldt 2020

ISBN 978 1 91351 919 3

Printed in Heshan, China

10 9 8 7 6 5 4 3 2 1

Contents

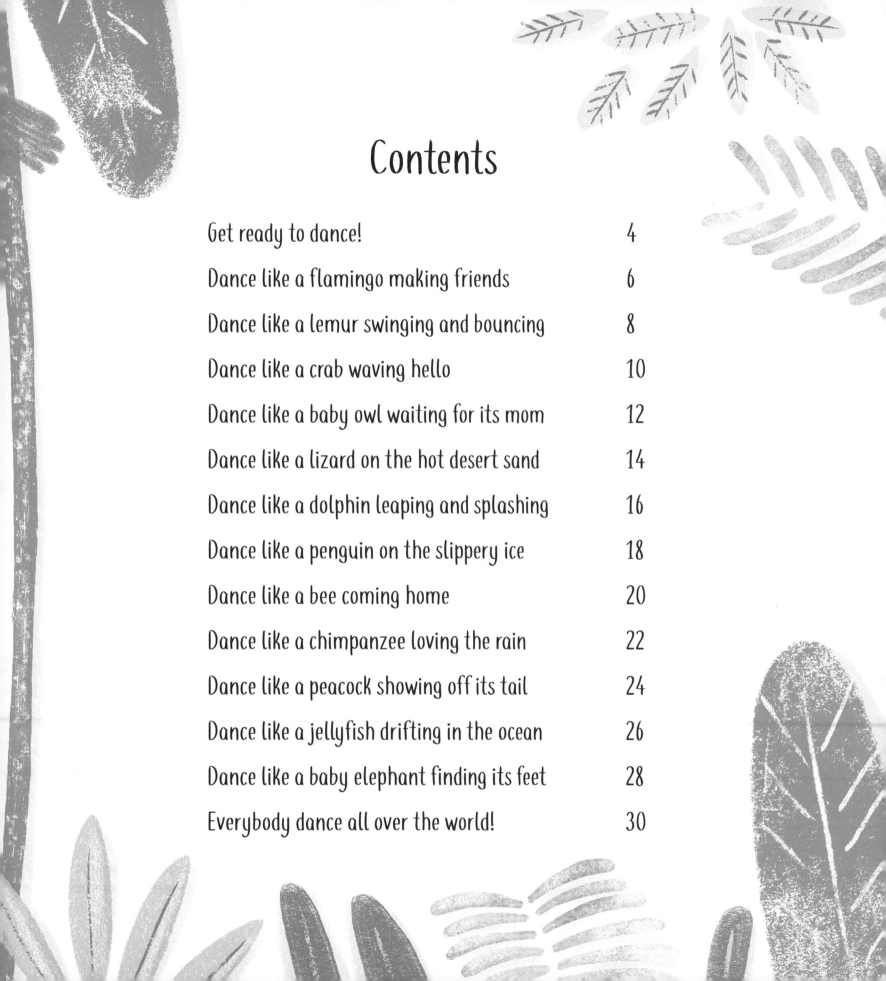

Hey little human,

do you want to move
like the wild animals of the world?
Get ready to stretch
and waggle and wave.
Get ready to wiggle and giggle and ...
dance!

Flamingoes live in a feathery crowd.
They wade through lakes on long stick legs,
dip-dip-dipping their beaks for food.
They like to show how beautiful they are,
to say "Come, build a nest with me."
Get ready to be a flashy flamingo and ...
dance!

Stretch up tall, fine flamingo.

Strut around. You're very proud.

Stretch out your wings to
show their color.

Take a bow.
What a beautiful bird!

Lemurs live in the leafy jungle.
They swing and spin like acrobats
leaping and bouncing between the trees,
looking for juicy fruit to eat,
then dozing and posing in the sun.
Get ready to do a lemur leap and ...
dance!

Crouch down ... then jump up!

Bounce, bounce along the ground.

Grab a piece of fruit to eat.

Now stretch out your arms.
It's time to sunbathe.

Crabs live on rocky beaches,
scuttling across the salty sand.
Some crabs like to wave their claws, to say
"I'm the biggest and the strongest.
Look at me! Look at me!"
Get ready to be a show-off crab and ...

dance!

Hold up your arms
like two strong claws.

Scuttle sideways, this way and that.

Wave a crab claw up and down.

Here comes a seagull.
Quickly! Hide!

Baby **Owls** sit on their branches
looking around at the world.
They fluff their feathers
and bob their heads.
Soon they'll fly for the very first time.
Get ready to be a baby owl and ...
dance!

Flap your arms to fluff up
your feathers.

Bob up and down, up and down.

Look both ways to see
what's what.

Time to fly, baby owl!

Little **Lizards** live in deserts.
They dart across the burning sand
looking for bugs to gobble up.
When they pause, they hoppity-hop
to stop their toes from getting hot.
Get ready to do the lizard hop and ...
dance!

Start out on your hands and knees.

Lift up your hands, one by one.

Lift up your feet, one by one.

Now do your moves over and over, faster and faster. That sand is hot!

Dolphins swim the salty seas
and love to play games in the waves.
They burst from the water like speedy
rockets, leaping up toward the sun.
Then SPLASH! They dive back down again.
Get ready to play a dolphin game and ...
dance!

Point your arms to make a beak.

Swim around in the water.

Jump up above the waves.

Then dive down to the seabed.

Penguins live in the southern seas.
They waddle around on the ice,
holding their flippers by their sides.
They rock along like wobbly toys,
trying not to slip and slide.
Get ready to do the penguin rock and ...
dance!

Hold your arms down by your sides.

Rock yourself from side to side.

Now rock around on the ice.

Wiggle your behind like a
penguin's tail.

When **Bees** fly home they do a dance,
a clever little wiggle-waggle that tells
the other bees where they've been.
It means "I found some lovely flowers.
My dance tells you which way to go."
Get ready to be a busy bee and ...
dance!

Fly around in a circle.

Wiggle your bottom.
Wiggle-waggle!

Point to where the flowers are.

Now fly off to find the flowers.

Chimpanzees love to dance
when it rains on their jungle home.
Raindrops drum down on the leaves.
Drum-drum. Splish-splash.
The louder the rain, the better the fun.
Get ready to be a happy chimp and ...
dance!

Clap your hands.
Here comes the rain.

Stamp your feet on the ground.

Wave your arms in the air.

Do your rain dance around
the jungle.

Have you seen a father **Peacock**
fanning out his marvelous tail?
His lovely feathers have shiny colors,
like the jewels on a crown.
Get ready to do the peacock strut and ...
dance!

Put your arms behind your back.

Now spread them like a peacock's tail.

Strut around to show off your feathers.

Close up your tail and nod your head. You are the perfect peacock!

Jellyfish jiggle and drift and sway,
this way, that way, beneath the waves.
Their tentacles trail like string in the sea.
Get ready to do the jellyfish jiggle and ...
dance!

Put your arms down by your sides.
Then wave them gently up and down.

Drift around in the ocean.
Keep waving your arms. Be slow, be calm.

Drift around faster in the waves.

Now do a super-shaky jiggle!

When baby **Elephants** are born
they're wibbly-wobbly on their feet.
They follow their moms,
wibble, wobble,
learning how to use their legs.
Get ready to do the elephant walk and ...
dance!

Get down on your hands
and knees.

Move around, swaying
your hips.

Pretend to go wobbly
like a baby ...

... and roll down into the mud!

Hey, **little human,** the world is wide.
There are lots more animals for you to see
and lots more moves for you to make.

Stretch up tall, reach down low,
wiggle wiggle, turn around,
and clap, clap, clap
for the **wonderful world!**